Discovering
the Guitar

DISCOVERING

DIAGRAMS BY GENE AZZAM

PHOTOGRAPHS BY KEITH DERRICKSON

William Morrow and Company
New York   1981

Linda
Swears

THE GUITAR

Teach
Yourself
to Play

Library of Congress Cataloging in Publication Data

Swears, Linda.
  Discovering the guitar.

  Includes index.
  Summary: Discusses the different types of guitars, how to buy one, tuning, reading a chord grid, and how to strum some basic chords. Includes lyrics and fingering for nineteen songs using seven basic chords.
  1. Guitar—Methods—Juvenile. [1. Guitar—Methods] I. Title.
MT801.G8S95   787.6′1   81-38335
ISBN 0-688-00717-1   AACR2
ISBN 0-688-00718-X (lib. bdg.)

TABLE OF CONTENTS

1

Before You Begin

H AVE YOU EVER WONDERED if you could learn to play the guitar? Well, you can. There is no magic involved. Learning to play the guitar takes time and effort, just like any other skill.

"Why are there so many different kinds of guitars?" "Which one is best for me?" "Do I have to read music to learn to play?" You will find answers to these questions as you read this book. You will learn a little history and plenty of facts about the guitar. You will learn to read a chord grid and even how to strum some basic chords. When you have finished this book, you will have a good background for further study on your own or with a guitar teacher.

Maybe you want to become a professional guitarist. Quite frankly, unless you are very talented indeed, the only way you will become a really good guitarist is to study with a qualified teacher. A guitar instructor can teach you to read music and help you develop more advanced techniques than will be covered in this book.

But maybe you just want to learn how to play for your own enjoyment. Maybe you would like to find out more about the guitar and see what you can do on your own. Whatever your goals may be, you have to start someplace, and helping you to get started is what this book is about.

2  The Modern Guitar

T HOUSANDS OF YEARS AGO people used the bow and arrow to hunt wild animals. Each time an arrow was released from the bow, the vibration of the string created a humming sound. This sound is probably the origin of the idea of making music from string vibrations. By adding strings of different lengths and thicknesses to the bow, the hunter's bow became a musical harp.

The sound of these early harps could be made louder by attaching a hollow gourd, tortoiseshell, or skull to the bow beneath the strings. With the addition of such a sound chamber, the first guitarlike instruments began to develop. For hundreds of years, people all over the world experimented with different combinations of strings and sound chambers to create musical sounds.

Then, about 700 years ago (A.D. 1200), the lute, an important ancestor of the guitar, became known in Europe. It had a pear-shaped wooden body with a sharply curved neck. Its strings ran from a bridge on the surface of the body, over a sound hole, and upward to a set of tuning pegs. One of the special features of the lute was its fretted neck. These frets were tiny strips of gut string tied around the fingerboard.

What is considered to be the first modern guitar did not appear until the mid 1800's, designed and built by a Spaniard named Antonio Torres Juardo. The basic style of this Spanish guitar is still popular today. It is called the classical guitar, and all modern

LUTE

guitars, from folk to electric, are variations of its design.

Today there are essentially three categories of modern guitars: classical, steel string, and electric. Because the classical guitar has the basic elements of all three, you can learn a lot about guitars in general by becoming acquainted with it first. As you read this section, look at the picture on page 17 frequently. Memorize the parts of this guitar now. Become familiar with how they help to produce musical sounds. This information will be very helpful when you select your first guitar and also when you begin to play.

Maybe you already have a guitar. If so, keep it handy as you read this chapter. How is it like the classical guitar? How is it different? To which category of guitars does it belong?

The classical guitar shown here is similar to the one built by Juardo over 100 years ago. It is usually made from spruce, maple, mahogany, or rosewood. Often it will have one type of wood for the surface of the body, another for the back, and still another for the neck. The use of various woods provides the beautiful contrast of colors found on different parts of many guitars.

As you look at the guitar, you will see the body is a curved wooden box with a sound hole cut into its surface. When the strings are plucked or strummed, the vibrations of the strings are transferred through the sound hole and ·the body. As the air inside the body vibrates along with the strings, the sound becomes amplified, or louder.

Notice that the strings of the guitar are not all alike. Three of them are thick and appear to be made of metal. While all the strings of the classical guitar are made of nylon, these three thicker strings are usually wrapped with wire. Because they are thick, they vibrate more slowly when they are plucked. The slower vibrations, in turn, make lower sounds.

Another reason these strings have a lower sound has to do with the tuning pegs found on the head of the guitar. Notice that each string of the guitar runs from the bridge to a tuning peg. By turning the peg, you can loosen or tighten a string. The tighter the string, the faster it vibrates and the higher its sound will be. If you loosen the guitar string, the string will vibrate more slowly and the sound will be lower.

One of the most important things for you to learn at this point is the name of each guitar string. Actually, each string has two names, a letter name and a number.

Looking at the picture of the classical guitar, notice the string to your far right is the first string E. It is the thinnest string, and when your guitar is properly tuned, it will make the highest sounds. The next string, from right to left, is the second string B, followed by third string G, fourth string D, fifth string A, and the sixth string E. Memorize these names now. You will need to know them to play even the simplest songs.

CLASSICAL GUITAR

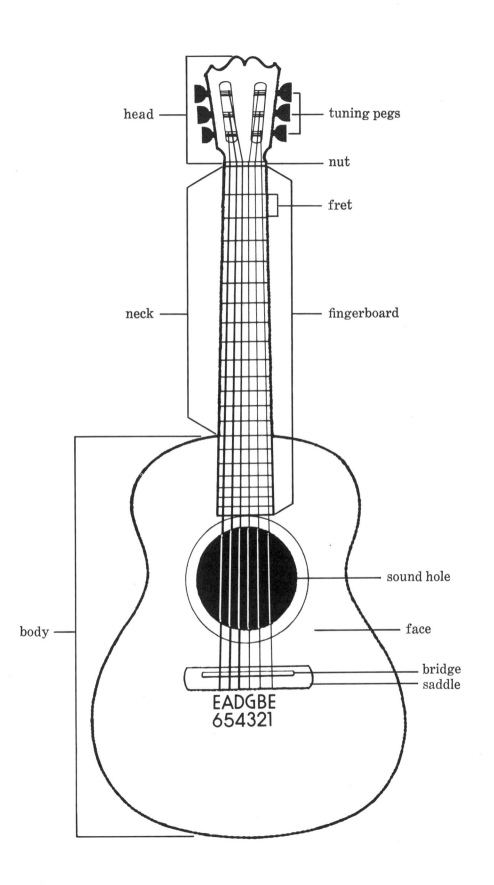

head

tuning pegs

nut

fret

neck

fingerboard

sound hole

face

body

bridge
saddle

EADGBE
654321

Follow each string up the neck of the guitar to the head where the tuning pegs are located. Discover which string is attached to which peg.

The neck of the guitar runs from the nut to the body. The nut is usually an etched piece of plastic located between the head and the neck. On top of the neck and running all the way to the sound hole is the fingerboard. You will notice that the fingerboard is divided by thin strips of metal. These strips are the frets. The first strip is the first fret, the second strip the second fret, the third strip the third fret, and so on. Although there are twelve frets on the neck of the classical guitar, you will need to know the location of only the first five for now.

There are some features of the classical guitar that differ from steel-string and electric models. It is usually lighter and easier to handle. It is always strung with nylon strings, helping to create a rich, mellow sound. The neck of the classical guitar is wider than the neck of other guitars. The strings are set farther apart, making them easier to pluck.

The classical guitar is the instrument played by the famous concert artist Andres Segovia. If you are not acquainted with this style of guitar playing, look for records by Segovia in your library or ask your librarian to help you find recordings by other classical guitarists like Julian Bream, John Williams, or Christopher Parkening. They are among the greatest guitarists in the world, and if you want to be a guitarist, you should be familiar with their music. A list of albums can be found on pages 91-92.

Of course, the classical guitar is not the only kind of guitar available. Steel-string guitars are very popular and come in every size and shape from the big western-jumbo to the small flattop student model. There seems to be a style of steel-string guitar to fit just about any musical taste, from jazz to country or rock.

The flattop is probably the most popular steel-string guitar. It has a long, slender neck with fourteen frets. The steel strings are strung closely together and are usually played with a pick. The head of the guitar is a solid piece of wood with steel shafts connected to the tuning pegs. There may be an additional tailpiece below the bridge.

While most steel-string guitars have a flat top and round sound hole, the f-hole is designed more like a violin. Although larger than a violin, it has an arched body and there are two f-shaped sound holes on its surface.

The twelve-string guitar is another type of steel-string guitar. For every string on the six-string guitar, this guitar has two. There are two low E's, two A's, two D's, two G's, two B's, and two higher E's. The resulting sound is fuller and richer, because there are more strings to vibrate.

At first, the twelve-string guitar might appear difficult to play. But the strings are strung closely together, and anyone who plays the six-string guitar can learn to play a twelve-string without too much trouble. However, it is not usually suggested for a beginner.

FLATTOP GUITAR

F-HOLE GUITAR

TWELVE-STRING GUITAR

Often a steel-string guitar will have a piece of plastic on its surface just below the sound hole. It protects the body from being damaged by the pick (also called "plectrum") as it is released from the strings. At one time, very expensive steel-string guitars had pick guards made of rare tortoiseshell.

Until the 1930's, all steel-string guitars were acoustical instruments. The word *acoustic* comes from the Greek for "heard," and any guitar that can be heard without electrical amplification is considered acoustic. All classical and many steel-string guitars are acoustical.

Around 1930, blues and jazz guitarists began to experiment by placing microphones under the strings of their guitars. The result was a louder, more resonant sound. Today some steel-string guitars come with an electrical hookup. They have volume and tone controls on the surface of a hollow body and can be played with or without electricity. For this reason, they are called "acoustical electric guitars."

If you are familiar with the solid-body electric guitar used by most rock groups, you've probably noticed it differs quite a bit from the diagram of the classical guitar. It has a long, thin fingerboard, and its body is cut away at the neck. This design enables the performer to play very high notes that could not be reached on a full-body guitar.

The solid-body electric guitar must be plugged in to be heard. It has no sound hole. Instead, the body is solid and houses electrical equipment that is con-

ACOUSTICAL
ELECTRIC GUITAR

SOLID-BODY
ELECTRIC GUITAR

nected to an amplifier and a speaker. When the guitar is played, the vibrations of the strings are transformed into electrical impulses. The amplifier picks up these impulses and converts them to sound. With added accessories like the fuzz box and the wah-wah pedal, these impulses can be altered. The wah-wah is popular for its "crybaby" effect, and the fuzz box can increase volume and adds a buzzing quality. The use of these accessories can create a wide variety of musical and, sometimes, not so musical sounds.

FUZZ BOX AND WAH-WAH PEDAL

3 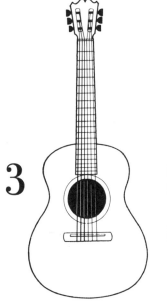 Selecting a Guitar

WITH ALL OF THESE GUITARS to choose from, which one is best for you? Most likely you will have the greatest success if you begin with a classical guitar. No matter what your goals may be, you first need to develop some basic guitar techniques. They can best be learned on a classical guitar.

Why? First of all, remember the classical guitar has nylon strings. These strings are much easier on the tender fingers of beginners than the metal strings of electric and steel-string guitars. When you are practicing, especially as a beginner, your fingers should not be sore.

Another reason for starting with the classical guitar is the distance between the strings. Sometimes beginners find it hard to keep each finger on just one string. Doing so is easier on the classical guitar because the strings are spaced a little farther apart on the fingerboard. Also you and those around you will find the sound of the classical guitar very pleasing. Playing an electric guitar with the volume turned up full blast is no way for a beginner to become popular with the neighbors.

If you are twelve or older, you can probably handle a full-size classical guitar without any trouble. However, if you are younger or if you have small hands, you may want to consider a three-quarter-size student guitar. These models have narrower necks and smaller bodies. They are excellent for young beginners, and many music shops will have them in stock.

A music shop is probably the best place for you to

FULL-SIZE AND THREE-QUARTER-SIZE CLASSICAL GUITARS

get your first guitar. You can buy guitars in many department stores and secondhand shops, but unless you know how to tell the quality of a guitar and how to tune one, your best bet is your local music store. Often a music store will have a wider variety of guitars from which to choose. Music dealers may be musicians themselves, and they will be able to help you select a quality instrument suited to your needs.

Some music stores have a student guitar rental policy, which usually allows you to rent a guitar for up to three months for a small fee—$25 to $35. At the end of the rental period, some dealers will apply your rental fee toward the purchase of the guitar. Renting is an excellent way to find out if your interest in playing the guitar is strong enough to make buying one worthwhile. If you have enjoyed playing and have practiced, buy your guitar. You should be able to get a suitable instrument for about $80 or $90. If you decide the guitar is not for you, you have not invested much money.

Another good reason for buying or renting your guitar at a music store is that someone there will be able to help you tune your instrument. Tuning the guitar can be the most difficult part of learning to play. To have your guitar tuned by a musician from the start is a big help.

A third reason for choosing your guitar at a music store is that many music shops have guitar teachers on the staff. They can teach you to read music and play more advanced guitar than will be covered in this book. Such a shop is likely to have a better selection of guitars, too, than one without a teacher. If the shop does not offer lessons, they may be able to suggest the name of a guitar instructor in your area.

Try calling several music shops and asking if they carry guitars and offer lessons before you actually go shopping. Look in the classified section of your telephone directory under *Musical Instruments* for the phone numbers and addresses of the shops in your area.

What if you already have a guitar? Look it over carefully. If it's not damaged and if it's properly strung, it can help you get started. If you are not sure about the condition of your guitar, ask a music teacher or someone who plays the guitar to inspect it for you.

Now, before you go off to the music store to select a guitar, here are a few things to look for:

1. Inspect the body of the guitar for scratches and dents. Make sure there are no cracks in the body or neck.
2. Check to see that the neck is straight and that the tuning pegs are not bent or damaged.
3. What is the overall construction of the guitar? Don't be afraid to ask the salesman why he feels one guitar is better than another. Often the reason will be because of the quality of wood and the construction of the instrument.
4. Hold the guitar. How does it feel? At first, just

about any guitar will feel awkward. That's because you've probably had very little experience holding one. Again a musician or salesperson can help you. If you are a young beginner, he may suggest a small-body guitar or he may help you decide you are able to handle a full-size instrument.

5. Be sure the strings of the guitar are not set too high off the fingerboard. The higher the strings, the more difficult they are to press down. Experiment by pressing the strings against the fingerboard with the fingers of your left hand. This movement should not be difficult.

6. How does the guitar sound? You should like the tone of the guitar, since you will be the person playing it.

4

Getting
Ready
to Play

F ROM THIS POINT ON, let's assume you have a guitar. If you don't, reading the next few sections of this book won't hurt you. But still, if you want to play the guitar, sooner or later you will have to rent, borrow, or buy one.

HOLDING THE GUITAR

Sit on an armless chair or stool. Your legs may be crossed or uncrossed, whichever is most comfortable for you. Carefully pick up the guitar, resting the neck in your left hand and the body on your right leg. Hold the guitar firmly against your body as shown in the picture. Bring your right arm over the

top of the guitar until your hand falls naturally over the sound hole. Place your left thumb behind the neck at about the second fret. Your wrist should be arched and the palm of your hand should not be touching the neck of the guitar. When you are playing, your fingertips will come around to press down the strings.

This holding position is recommended for all beginners. Whether you are left-handed or right-handed, you will still rest the body of the guitar on your right leg and the neck in your left hand.

HOLDING A PICK

If you have a steel-string guitar and you want to use a pick to strum, be sure you hold it correctly. Rest the pick on the first joint of your right index finger. Make sure the point of the pick is facing away from your hand. Gently place your thumb over the

top of the pick and you are ready to strum. (Generally a pick is not used with a classical guitar.)

STRUMMING

The easiest strum to learn is simply moving the thumb of your right hand in a downward motion over the strings. Keep your right hand in a slightly curved position as you strum. Your thumb should be almost parallel to the strings.

Go ahead, now that your guitar is in proper position, and try a few strums! How does it feel? In the beginning, holding and playing the guitar may seem very awkward. Don't be discouraged. Trying something new usually does feel strange at first.

How does the guitar sound? Unless someone has tuned it for you, it probably sounds pretty bad. To make music with a guitar, each string must sound a certain pitch. Musicians say it must be "in tune."

WHAT IS TUNING?

Tuning your guitar simply means to adjust each string to a certain tension. The different tensions will result in different pitches for each string. The word *pitch* refers to how high or low the string will sound when it is plucked.

Will a string with a loose tension have a high pitch or a low pitch? The answer is that it will sound a low pitch, because the looser tension causes the string to vibrate more slowly. The slower the vibrations, the lower the pitch will be.

If you don't understand this concept, take a few minutes to experiment with a rubber band before you experiment with your guitar.

Place a rubber band over a door knob, and pull it down with one thumb. With the index finger of your other hand, pluck the rubber band, causing it to vibrate. Continue to pull the rubber band tighter as you pluck. You will notice two things happening. First, the sound becomes higher as the tightness, or tension, of the string is increased. Second, the appearance of the rubber band changes. It becomes thinner and vibrates more quickly.

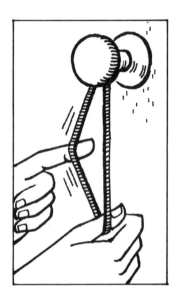

This principle is the one that governs tuning a guitar. To be "in tune," each string must be adjusted to just the right tension.

Besides understanding what tuning is, you need to begin to develop the musical skill of matching pitches. You will be learning to listen carefully to musical pitches and how to reproduce them with your own voice.

You can develop this skill in many ways. When you listen to a record and sing along, you are actually matching many pitches with the voice or instruments on the recording. When you sing with friends at school or church, you are matching pitches with other singers. When you play a tune on the piano and hum along, you are matching pitches with the piano.

You will need to be able to match pitches with the guitar in order to tune your instrument and to sing along as you play. Here's a little exercise that will help you develop this skill and also help you become more familiar with the guitar fingerboard.

Place your guitar in proper holding position. With your left index finger, press down the second string B at the first fret. With your right thumb, pluck the B string over the sound hole several times. Now sing that pitch on lu, la, or any syllable easy for you to sing. Experiment until your voice is sounding exactly the same pitch as the guitar. Repeat the same procedure by pressing down and plucking:

1. first string E, third fret
2. first string E, second fret
3. first string E, first fret
4. first string E, open
   ("Open" means the string is not pressed down by a finger of the left hand. The whole string is allowed to vibrate.)

Did you notice the pitches of the E string becoming lower as your left hand moved toward the nut? Not only does the tension and thickness of a string affect its pitch; the length of a string is also important. When your finger stops the string at a certain fret, it functions to shorten the string. The part of the string between your finger and the nut no longer vibrates. Now only the portion of the string from the bridge to where the string is stopped will vibrate. The shorter the vibrating portion, the higher the pitch.

Experiment moving your fingers up and down the fingerboard. Create high and low pitches by stopping the strings at different frets. Can you match these pitches with your voice?

TUNING THE GUITAR

Because a properly tuned guitar is so important, several different methods of tuning will be given here. Use the one that is best for you. If you have trouble tuning, don't be discouraged. Learning to tune the guitar takes time and practice, just like learning to play.

First, make sure your guitar is in tune from the start by having it tuned at the music store or by someone who plays guitar. Unfortunately, guitars don't stay in tune forever, especially new ones. So you must learn to tune your own instrument. Before you begin any practice session, always check to see that your guitar is in tune. The easiest way is to use six notes of the piano keyboard. If a piano isn't available, there are several other methods you may use. However, read this section first. The principles of tuning your guitar to the piano can be applied to other tuning procedures.

Sit at the piano holding your guitar in correct playing position. Starting with the lowest tone of the piano (A), count up to the twelfth white note and play it with your left hand. Think the pitch in your mind. With your right hand, pluck the sixth string E of the guitar. If the two pitches sound exactly the same, your sixth string E is in tune. However, if the sixth string E sounds higher than the E of the piano, gradually turn the tuning peg to loosen the string. To be sure you turn the correct peg, move your left index finger up the string until it meets the tuning peg. Slowly turn the peg and pluck the sixth string E until it matches the pitch of the E of the piano. If the sixth string E sounds lower than the E of the piano, gradually tighten the string until the two sounds match.

At first, it may be hard to tell if the sound of your guitar strings are higher or lower than those of the piano, so don't take a chance on breaking a string. As a general rule, always lower the pitch of a guitar string until you are sure it is lower than the piano pitch. Then begin to increase the tension of the strings.

Now continue. Using the diagram on the next page, tune each string of the guitar to its corresponding note on the piano.

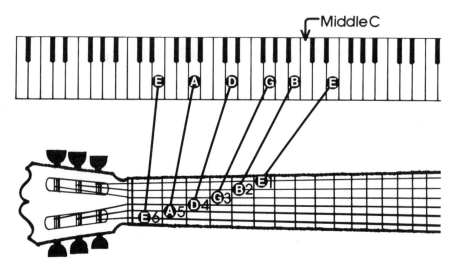

TUNING WITH THE PIANO

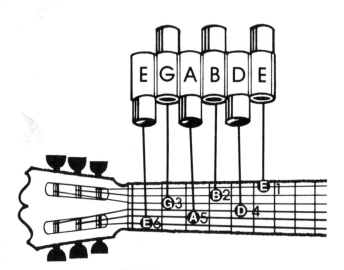

TUNING WITH THE PITCH PIPE

If you don't have access to a piano, you can purchase an inexpensive guitar pitch pipe to help you
tune. It is a small set of tiny pipes connected by a

metal brace. The guitar can be tuned to these pipes using the same procedure as given for tuning to the piano.

Two other ways of tuning are to a special guitar-tuning record that can be purchased for a few dollars at a music store and to a tape recording. If you have a tape recorder and if you are sure your guitar is in tune, record the sound of each string and then play the tape back whenever you need to tune.

Sometimes you will hear guitarists talk about "string to string tuning." This method requires very careful listening, and it is not recommended for beginners. If you decide to take lessons, your teacher will explain this method of tuning.

Don't be discouraged if you have trouble hearing whether pitches are higher or lower. You are not alone! This problem is a common one for beginners. For some people, tuning is the most difficult part of learning to play. As you work with the guitar you will begin to develop a better "ear," and tuning will become easier each time you do it.

There are just two things you need to know before you are ready to play your first chords. They are left-hand fingering and how to read a chord grid.

FINGERING FOR THE LEFT HAND

Look at the palm side of your left hand. Starting with your index finger, each finger has a number.

Your index finger is number one, middle finger number two, ring finger number three, and little finger number four. You will need to know the number for each finger to read a chord grid.

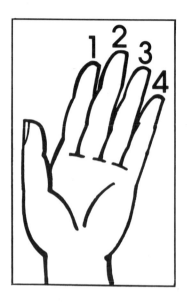

READING A CHORD GRID

What is a chord grid? It's a picture, a diagram that usually represents the part of the fingerboard closest to the nut and shows you what your left hand should be doing. Here's a chord grid for the D chord.

The circles on this grid show you where your fingers should be placed. The numbers inside the circles tell you which finger to use. If there is an X above a string, don't strum that string. If there is an *O* above the string, the string is strummed, but the left hand does not press on the string. The *O* stands for "open string."

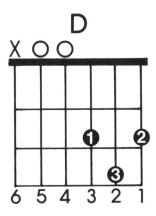

As you can see from the chord grid, playing a chord means playing a cluster of musical pitches at once. These clusters are called "harmony." By changing chords, or harmonies, as you strum the guitar, you can create accompaniments to familiar songs.

5

Playing
the Guitar

THE THREE-STRING
C AND G7 CHORDS

You're ready to play! The first chord you will learn is the three-string C chord.

Holding your guitar in the correct position, stop the second string B just behind the first fret with your left index finger (number 1). Strum the third, second, and first strings with the thumb of your right hand. You've just played your first chord!

The second chord is the three-string G7 chord. Place your index finger on the first string just behind the first fret. Strum the third, second, and first strings with the thumb of your right hand.

Now practice changing from C to G7:

C   C   C   C   G7   G7   G7   G7   C   C   C   C

When you can play this pattern without pausing or looking at your hands, you're ready for your first song.

Look at the first three songs in this book. Select the one you know best. Your voice will be carrying the melody as you accompany yourself, so you will have to know the song. To find the first note of the song, pluck the string indicated and match your voice with that pitch. It will give you the correct starting pitch. Sing the song through once.

Sing the song again. This time whenever you see the chord symbol *C* written above a word, finger C and strum. When you see *G7*, finger G7 and strum.

Three-String C
X X X O O

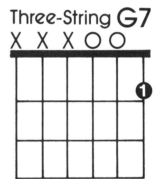

Three-String G7
X X X O O

SONGS USING
THE THREE-STRING C AND G7 CHORDS

Row, Row, Row Your Boat

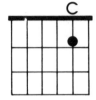

Starting note:
Match your voice
to the second string
stopped at the first fret.

```
C    C   C        C
Row, row, row your boat,
C       C       C       C
gent-ly down the stream,—
C          C          C          C
mer-ri-ly, mer-ri-ly, mer-ri-ly, mer-ri-ly,
G7   G7   C    C
life is but a dream.—
```

Rock-a My Soul

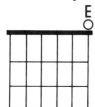

Starting note:
Match your voice
to the open first string.

C   C   C   C
Rock-a my soul in the bos-om of A-bra-ham,
G7   G7   G7   G7
rock-a my soul in the bos-om of A-bra-ham,
C   C   C   C
rock-a my soul in the bos-om of A-bra-ham,
G7 G7 C C
oh,—rock-a my soul.—

He's Got the Whole World in His Hands

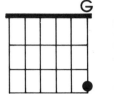

Starting note:
Match your voice
to the first string
stopped at the third fret.

         C   **C**   **C**   **C**
He's got the whole world in His hands,
         G7   **G7**   **G7**   **G7**
He's got the whole world in His hands,
         C   **C**   **C**   **C**
He's got the whole world in His hands,
         G7   **G7** **C**   **C**
He's got the whole world in His hands.—

2. He's got the wind and the rain in His hands.

3. He's got you and me, brother, in His hands.

4. He's got the little bitty baby in His hands.

5. He's got everybody in His hands.

THE COMPLETE C AND G7 CHORDS

The chords you have learned so far are simplified versions of the C and G7 chords. If you are comfortable with these chords and can move smoothly from one to the other, keeping the beat steady, you are ready to learn the complete C and G7 chords. You will notice that these chords use more strings and, therefore, they make a fuller and more interesting sound.

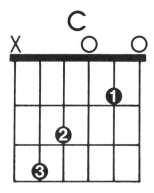

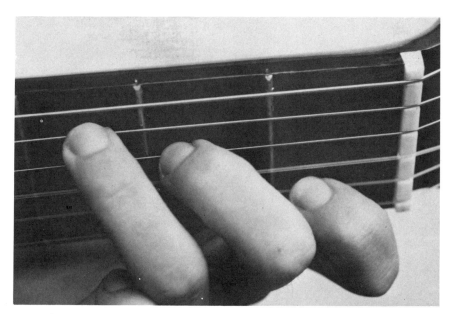

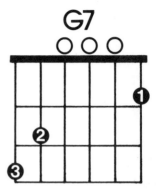

G7

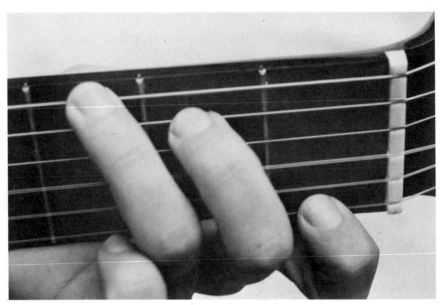

At first this new fingering will seem awkward and hard to reach. But the more you practice the easier it will become. Once you have learned to move from C to G7 and back again, all the other chords can be learned more quickly. So spend some time getting these two basic chords down pat.

Practice using the exercises below. The straight lines are beat marks. Strum each time you see a beat mark, and keep the beats steady even when you're changing chords. Remember to keep your right hand slightly curved and to strum with your thumb in a downward motion over the sound hole. Begin slowly.

STRUM PRACTICE

C   G7   C   G7
1. / / / / / / / / / / / / / / / /

C   G7   C   G7   C
2. / / / / / / / / / / / / / / /

C G7 C G7 C G7 C G7
3. / / / / / / / / / / / / / / / /

C G7 C G7 C G7 C G7 C
4. / / / / / / / / /

When you begin to feel comfortable with these chords (you may need a few days), review the first songs in this book using the complete chords. When you've learned them, go on to the next three songs.

SONGS USING
THE COMPLETE C AND G7 CHORDS

Skip to My Lou

E
○

Starting note:
Match your voice
to the open first string.

C   /   /   /
Flies in the but-ter-milk, shoo fly shoo,
G7   /   /   /
Flies in the but-ter-milk, shoo fly shoo,
C   /   /   /
Flies in the but-ter-milk, shoo fly shoo,
G7   /   C   /
Skip to my lou, my dar - ling.

Refrain
C   /   /   /
Skip, skip, skip to my lou,
G7   /   /   G7
Skip, skip, skip to my lou,
C   /   /   /
Skip, skip, skip to my lou,
G7   /   C   /
Skip to my lou, my dar - ling.

2. Little red wagon painted blue,

3. Lost my partner, what'll I do?

4. I'll get another one better than you,

Oh, My Darling Clementine

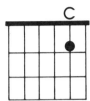

Starting note:
Match your voice
to the second string
stopped at the first fret.

   C   **/**
In a ca-vern, in a can-yon,
    C   **G7**
ex-ca-va-ting for a mine,
  G7   **C**
dwelt a min-er, for-ty-nin-er,
   G7   **C**
and his daugh-ter Clem-en-tine.

Refrain
     C   **/**
Oh, my dar-ling, oh, my dar-ling,
    C   **G7**
oh, my dar-ling Clem-en-tine,
   G7   **C**
you are gone and lost for-ev-er,
    G7   **C**
dread-ful sor-ry, Clem-en-tine.

2. Light she was and like a fairy,
   and her shoes were number nine.
   Herring boxes, without topses,
   sandals were for Clementine.
Refrain

3. Drove she ducklings to the water,

every morning just at nine.
Stubbed her toe upon a splinter,
fell into the foaming brine.

Refrain

4. Ruby lips above the water,
   blowing bubbles soft and fine.
   But, alas! I was no swimmer,
   so I lost my Clementine.

Refrain

5. There's a churchyard, on the hillside,
   where the flowers grow and twine.
   There grow roses, 'mongst the posies,
   fertilized by Clementine.

Refrain

Frère Jacques

Starting note:
Match your voice
to the second string
stopped at the first fret.

C   G7 C   /   /   G7 C   /
Are you sleep-ing, are you sleep-ing,
C   G7 C   / /   G7 C   /
Broth-er John,— Broth-er John?—
C   G7   C   /
Morn-ing bells are ring-ing,
C   G7   C   /
morn-ing bells are ring-ing,
C   G7   C   /
ding, ding, dong;—
C   G7   C   /
ding, ding, dong.—

THE F CHORD

This F chord is called a "small bar chord," which means that one of your fingers must press down two strings at the same time. In this case, your index finger presses down both the first and second strings. Some people feel the F chord is difficult to play for this reason. However, as you learn to play the F chord, you will not only be developing bar technique, you will be learning a chord that is often used.

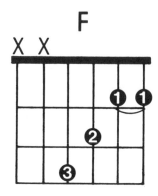

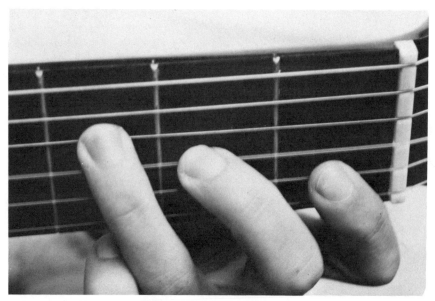

Experiment with the fingering shown here. Be sure not to let the palm of your hand touch the neck of the guitar. To avoid a buzzing sound with this chord, move the side of your index finger just to the edge of the first fret.

Here are some exercises to help you learn moving back and forth from the F chord.

STRUM PRACTICE

C	F	C	F	C

1. /

C	F	C	G7	C

2. /

C	G7	C	F	C

3. /

SONGS USING
THE C, G7, AND F CHORDS

Oh, Susanna

Starting note:
Match your voice
to the second string
stopped at the first fret.

```
    C        /   /   /   /   /      G7  /
I come from Al-a-ba-ma with a ban-jo on my knee,—
      C      /     /   / /      G7  C  /
I'm goin' to Lou-'si-an-a, my true love for to see.—
      C        /        /   /      /
It rain'd all night the day I left, the weath-er
   /    G7  /
   it was dry,—
      C    /   /      /
the sun so hot I froze to death,
      /     G7     C  /
   Su-san-na, don't you cry.—
F  /  /    /   C       /     G7 /
Oh, Su-san-na, oh, don't you cry for me;—
   C        /   /   /   /     G7   C   /
I come from Al-a-ba-ma with a ban-jo on my knee.—
```

2. I had a dream the other night
      when everything was still.
   I thought I saw Susanna dear,
      a-comin' down the hill.

The buckwheat cake was in her mouth,
   a tear was in her eye.
Said I, "I'm coming from the South.
   Susanna, don't you cry."
Oh, Susanna, oh, don't you cry for me;
I come from Alabama with a banjo on my knee.

On Top of Old Smoky

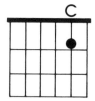

Starting note:
Match your voice
to the second string
stopped at the first fret.

```
    C        F     / /
On top of Old Smo - ky,—
    F          C    / /
all cov-ered with snow,——
    C          G7   / /
I lost my true lov - er,—
    G7          C   / /
for court-ing too slow.——
```

2. Oh, courting's a pleasure,
   but parting's a grief,
   and a falsehearted lover,
   is worse than a thief.

3. A thief will but rob you
   of all that you save,
   but a falsehearted lover
   sends you to your grave.

4. The grave will decay you
   and turn you to dust,
   but a falsehearted lover
   you never can trust.

Silent Night

Starting note:
Match your voice
to the first string
stopped at the third fret.

```
C     /   /   /
```
Si-lent night, ho-ly night,
```
G7  /    C   /
```
all is calm, all is bright,
```
F        /       C          /
```
round yon Vir-gin, Moth-er and Child,
```
F   /        C          /
```
ho-ly in-fant so ten-der and mild,
```
G7       /          C    /
```
sleep in heav-en-ly peace,—
```
C     G7       C   /
```
sleep in heav-en-ly peace.—

2. Silent night, holy night,
   shepherds quake at the sight.
   Glories stream from heaven afar.
   Heavenly hosts sing "Alleluia,
   Christ the Savior is born!
   Christ the Savior is born!"

3. Silent night, holy night,
   Son of God, love's pure light
   radiant beams from Thy holy face,
   with the dawn of redeeming grace,
   Jesus, Lord, at Thy birth,
   Jesus, Lord, at Thy birth!

Swing Low, Sweet Chariot

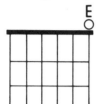

E

Starting note:
Match your voice
to the open first string.

Refrain
```
        C  /      F    C
Swing low,— sweet char-i-ot,
C            /      G7   /
com-in' for to car-ry me home.—
        C  /      F    C
Swing low,— sweet char-i-ot,
C            G7       C   /
com-in' for to car-ry me home.—
```

```
     C          /        /        /
1. I looked o-ver Jor-dan and what did I see,
     C          /      G7    /
   com-in' for to car-ry me home?—
      C     /      /          /
   A band of an-gels, com-in' af-ter me,
   C          G7       C   /
   com-in' for to car-ry me home.—
```
                                   Refrain

2. If you get there before I do,
   comin' for to carry me home,
   just tell my friends I'm comin' too,
   comin' for to carry me home.
                                   Refrain

3. Sometimes I'm up and sometimes down,
   comin' for to carry me home,
   but still my soul feels heavenly bound,
   comin' for to carry me home.

                    Refrain

6 Playing by Ear

HAVE YOU EVER heard the expression, "She plays by ear"? Usually it refers to someone who plays a musical instrument without reading musical notation. Learning to play "by ear" is a skill just like learning to read music. It takes practice and concentration.

With the three chords you have learned so far, you can accompany many songs. But what if a song you want to sing is not in this book? Well, you could try to find it in another book and hope it uses the C, G7, and F chords, or you could try to play it by ear using the chords you've learned. You can't accompany all songs with these chords, but here are a few that will work out nicely:

"Michael, Row the Boat Ashore"
"Kum Ba Yah"
"Good Night, Ladies"

At first, playing by ear is really a matter of guessing when chord changes occur and what chords to use. After you've practiced a little, you may find you begin to "feel," or sense, the chord changes. Not everyone is able to develop this skill. But who knows? Maybe you can. You won't know unless you try.

Choose one of the songs listed here, and follow these three suggestions to get started:

1. Start and end the song with the C chord.
2. Usually follow a G7 or F chord with a C chord.

3. The next to last chord will most likely be a G7.

Don't give up if you don't have instant success. For some, playing by ear will seem very natural. Whatever your ability seems to be, attempting to play by ear is good training for any musician.

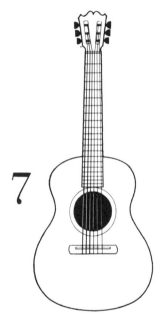

7 More Chords
and Songs

THE NEW CHORDS
D AND A7

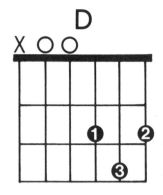

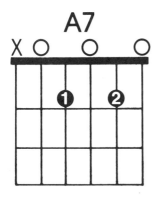

A7

STRUM PRACTICE

   D   A7   D   A7   D
1. / / / / / / / / / / / / / / / /

   D   A7   D   A7   D   A7
2. / / / / / / / / / / / / / / / /

   D A7 D A7 D A7 D A7 D
3. / / / / / / / / / / / / / / / /

SONGS USING
THE D AND A7 CHORDS

Down in the Valley

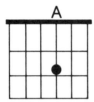

Starting note:
Match your voice
to the third string
stopped at the second fret.

D / / / **A7** /
Down in the val - ley,   val-ley so low,—
A7 / / / **D** /
hang your head o - ver,   hear the wind blow.—
D / / / **A7** /
Hang your head o - ver,   hear the wind blow.—
A7 / / / **D** /
Hang your head o - ver,   hear the wind blow.

2. Roses love sunshine, violets love dew.
   Angels in heaven know I love you,
   know I love you, dear, know I love you.
   Angels in heaven know I love you.

3. Writing a letter containing three lines,
   asking a question, will you be mine?
   Will you be mine, dear, will you be mine?
   Asking a question, will you be mine?

Pay Me My Money Down

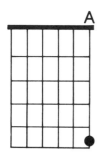

Starting note:
Match your voice
to the first string
stopped at the fifth fret.

D   /   /   /
I thought I heard the captain say,
D   /   **A7**   /
  "Pay me my mo-ney down.
  A7   /   /   /
To-mor-row is our sail-ing day,
A7   /   **D**   /
  pay me my mo-ney down."

Refrain
D /   / /
"Pay me, oh, pay me,
D   /   **A7**   /
  pay me my mo-ney down.
A7 /   /   /
Pay me or go to jail,
A7   /   **D**   /
  pay me my mo-ney down."

2. As soon as the boat was clear of the bar,
   "Pay me my money down,"
   he knocked me down with the end of a spar,
   "Pay me my money down."
                    Refrain

3. Well, I wish I was Mr. Steven's son.
   "Pay me my money down,"
   Sit on the bank and watch the work done,
   "Pay me my money down."

   Refrain

Here's a song you learned to play using the C and G7 chord. When you play it using the D and A7 chords, it will sound a little higher.

Rock-a My Soul

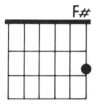

Starting note:
Match your voice
to the first string
stopped at the second fret.

D / / /
Rock-a my soul in the bos-om of A-bra-ham,
A7 / / /
rock-a my soul in the bos-om of A-bra-ham,
D / / /
rock-a my soul in the bos-om of A-bra-ham,
A7 / **D** /
oh,— rock-a my soul.—

THE NEW CHORD G

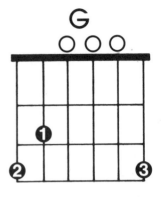

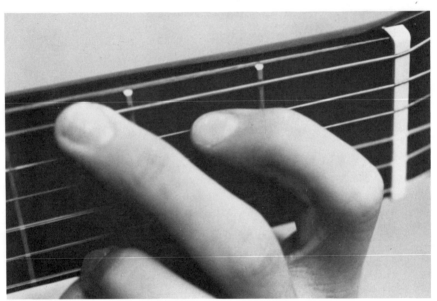

STRUM PRACTICE

```
    D       G       D       G       D
1. / / / / / / / / / / / / / / / / / / / /

    D       G       D       A7      D
2. / / / / / / / / / / / / / / / / / / / /

    D       A7      D       G       D
3. / / / / / / / / / / / / / / / / / / / /
```

SONGS USING
THE D, A7, AND G CHORDS

Michael, Row the Boat Ashore

Starting note:
Match your voice
to the second string
stopped at the third fret.

D / / / / **G / D**
Mich-ael, row the boat a-shore, hal-le-lu - ia,
D / / **A7** / **D A7 D**
Mich-ael, row the boat a-shore, hal-le-lu - ia.

2. Noah was a gentle man, halleluia.

3. Gabriel, blow the trumpet strong, halleluia.

4. Brother, help me turn the wheel, halleluia.

Kum Ba Ya

Starting note:
Match your voice
to the second string
stopped at the third fret.

D   **/**   **/**   **/ G**   **D / /**
Kum ba ya, my Lord,— kum ba ya.——
D   **/**   **/**   **/ /**   **A7/ /**
Kum ba ya, my Lord,— kum ba ya.——
A7   **D**   **/**   **/ G**   **D / /**
Kum ba ya, my Lord,— kum ba ya.——
D   **/**   **/ / A7**   **D / /**
Oh, Lord,— kum ba ya.——

2. Someone's crying, Lord, kum ba ya.

3. Someone's singing, Lord, kum ba ya.

4. Someone's praying, Lord, kum ba ya.

Good Night, Ladies

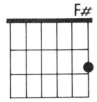

Starting note:
Match your voice
to the first string
stopped at the second fret.

D / / /
Good night, la-dies,
D / **A7** /
good night, la-dies,
D / **G** /
good night, la-dies,
    D   **A7**   **D** /
we're going to leave you now.—

Refrain
D / / /
Mer-ri-ly we roll a-long,
A7 / **D** /
roll a-long, roll a-long,
D / / /
mer-ri-ly we roll a-long,
A7 / **D** /
o'er the deep blue sea.—

2. Sweet dreams, ladies,
   sweet dreams, ladies,
   sweet dreams, ladies,
   we're going to leave you now.
                    Refrain

I've Been Working on the Railroad

G

Starting note:
Match your voice
to the first string
stopped at the third fret.

```
G        /              /   /
I've been work-ing on the rail-road
C    /      G   /
all the live-long day ;—
G        /              /   /
I've been work-ing on the rail-road
   A7     /    D   /
to pass the time a-way.—
D         /              G    /
Can't you hear the whis-tle blow-ing?
C          /          G    /
Rise up so ear-ly in the morn.—
C          /              G     /
Can't you hear the cap-tain shout-ing,
  G     D       G    /
"Di-nah, blow your horn."—

G                 /      C                    /
Di-nah, won't you blow,   Di-nah, won't you blow,
D                 /          G   /
Di-nah, won't you blow your horn?—
G                 /      C                    /
Di-nah, won't you blow,   Di-nah, won't you blow,
D                 /          G   /
Di-nah, won't you blow your horn?—
```

G   /   / /
Some-one's in the kit-chen with Di - nah,
G   /   D /
some-one's in the kit-chen I know.—
G   /   C /
Some-one's in the kit-chen with Di - nah,
D   / G /
strum-ming on the old ban-jo, a sing-ing

G / /   /
Fee, fi, fid-dly-i-o,
G /   D /
fee, fi, fid-dly-i-o-o-o-o,
G / C   /
fee, fi, fid-dly-i-o,
D   / G /
strum-ming on the old ban-jo.—

THE NEW CHORD Em

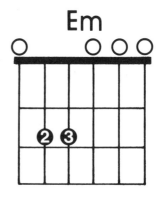

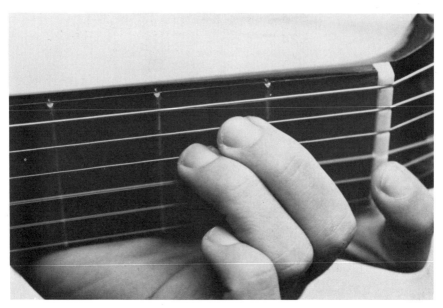

By adding the Em chord to the chords you already know, you will bring greater interest to your music. Begin by adding the Em chord to the songs "Michael, Row the Boat Ashore" and "Kum Ba Ya."

SONGS USING
THE D, A7, G, AND Em CHORDS

Michael, Row the Boat Ashore

Starting note:
Match your voice
to the second string
stopped at the third fret.

D / / / / **G** / **D**
Mich-ael, row the boat a-shore, hal-le-lu - ia,
D / / **Em** / **D A7 D**
Mich-ael, row the boat a-shore, hal-le-lu - ia.

2. Noah was a gentle man, halleluia.

3. Gabriel, blow the trumpet strong, halleluia.

4. Brother, help me turn the wheel, halleluia.

Kum Ba Ya

Starting note:
Match your voice
to the second string
stopped at the third fret.

D   /   /   / G   D / /
Kum ba ya, my Lord,— kum ba ya.——
D   /   /   / Em   A7/ /
Kum ba ya, my Lord,— kum ba ya.——
A7   D   /   / G   D / /
Kum ba ya, my Lord,— kum ba ya.——
Em D / / A7   D / /
Oh, Lord,— kum ba ya.——

2. Someone's crying, Lord, kum ba ya.

3. Someone's singing, Lord, kum ba ya.

4. Someone's praying, Lord, kum ba ya.

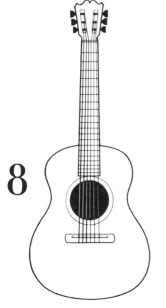

8 Learning More About the Guitar

THE CHORDS YOU HAVE LEARNED in this book are just the beginning of all there is to know about playing the guitar. There are hundreds of chords not mentioned here. You can learn many of them through guitar manuals available at most music shops and some libraries. If your goal is simply to be able to accompany familiar songs and if you have a good ear, these manuals are helpful.

Is there a guitar club at your school? Exchanging chords and strum patterns with friends is another way of learning more. Does your school offer a guitar class? Investigate!

If you have the notion you would like to be a fine guitarist, there is no substitute for study with a qualified teacher. If you want to play in a band or hope to become a professional guitarist, contact a teacher now.

Ask your music teacher at school to suggest a guitar instructor, or perhaps there is one on the staff of a college near you. Some college instructors will give private lessons to serious young students. Call the music department of the college, ask for the guitar instructor, and find out. Is there a guitar instructor at a music shop near you?

If you are unable to find a teacher in this way or through the recommendation of another guitarist, look in the classified advertisements in your telephone directory under *Music Instructor*. Guitar teachers will be listed there.

Listening to guitar music is another important way of learning about the instrument. Here is a list of recordings to help you get started. Each highlights the talents of a famous guitarist. If these records are not available through your library, ask the librarian to suggest others by the same artists. As you listen, you may discover guitar styles you've never heard before. Perhaps you'll find another style you would like to play.

SUGGESTED LISTENING

CLASSICAL
Andres Segovia: *Three Centuries of Guitar*
Andres Segovia: *The Guitar and I*
John Williams: *John Williams*
Julian Bream: *Baroque Guitar*
Christopher Parkening: *The Christopher Parkening Album*

BLUES
John Lee Hooker: *The Real Blues*
Lightnin' Hopkins: *Blues*
B.B. King: *Lucille*

JAZZ
Charlie Byrd: *Let It Be*
Wes Montgomery: *The Best of Wes Montgomery*

COUNTRY
Chet Atkins: *Country Pickin'*
Doc Watson: *Elementary, Doctor Watson*

ROCK
Eric Clapton: *Wheels of Fire*
George Harrison: *All Things Must Pass*
Jimi Hendrix: *In the West*
Led Zeppelin: *Led Zeppelin II*

9

Caring for Your Guitar

T HE GUITAR IS a delicate instrument. It needs protection from bumps and sudden changes in temperature. One of the best safeguards against both of these problems is a guitar case of heavy construction. Always carry your guitar in this type of case to prevent bent tuning pegs, popped strings, and scratches on the body.

Extreme temperatures can also damage a guitar. Heat will often warp the guitar while cold temperatures will make it brittle and cause the wood to split. If your guitar should get damp, wipe it dry before returning it to its case.

If you are going to store your guitar for a while, find a place where it will not be exposed to extreme temperatures. Always loosen the strings before storage to prevent warping of the neck.

As a general rule, never carry your guitar in the trunk of a car. The extreme temperatures and rough ride will ruin it in no time!

Index
of Songs